THE LOGIC OF LIFE

The Logic of Life

R.C. Nisbon

The Logic of Life

Seeking truth to live by

P.G. NELSON

AVENUE BOOKS

First published 2008

Published by Avenue Books
c/o P.O. Box 2118, Seaford BN25 9AR.

ISBN: 978 1 905575 04 6

Book design and production for the publisher by
Bookprint Creative Services, <www.bookprint.co.uk>
Printed in Great Britain.

CONTENTS

CHAPTER ONE

INTRODUCTION

We all need truth. When I was a child I learnt that, if I let go of a heavy object, it would fall. This would be painful if it fell on my foot. Since then I have been using this lesson in practical situations, almost without thinking about it.

I had learnt a "truth". If someone lets go of a heavy object, it falls. Whoever the person is, wherever he or she may be in the world, the object falls. It can only be stopped by applying a sufficient force in the opposite direction.

Truths of this kind form the basis of modern science. Scientists make observations, establish relations between them, and devise theories to explain them. Some theories are very speculative (e.g. those relating to the origin of the universe). Others explain large numbers of observations, and are correspondingly more certain.[1]

Applied scientists use scientific knowledge to provide practical solutions to problems in many areas of life. Some of these are controversial, either because the science on which they are based is uncertain, or because of other considerations.

Most, however, we gladly accept, from flying in an aeroplane to having an anaesthetic at the dentist. Many we take for granted.

There are, however, areas of life where science cannot help. John is married with three children. At work he meets Sally to whom he is attracted. He would like to leave his wife and live with Sally. Sally would like this too. Is there a truth to guide John and Sally in this situation?

Again, Peter is single, he has lost his job, and his doctor has told him that he has an incurable disease. He feels like taking his life. "What's the point of living?" he tells a friend. Is there a truth for this situation?

This book is about possible truths of this kind. Are there such truths, and if there are, where can they be found?

I begin by taking a step back. Behind these questions are more fundamental issues. I look at these first.

CHAPTER TWO

KEY QUESTIONS

When I look up at the sky on a clear night, I can see the stars in their constellations. On a very clear night, in open country, I can see the Milky Way. Astronomers tell me that this is made up of a hundred billion stars, including the sun, arranged in a huge spiral, and constituting a galaxy. They also tell me that many of the other sources of light that I can see are actually galaxies, and that there are about a hundred billion galaxies. I stand in wonder.

I also stand in wonder when I view a landscape, and when I look at plants and animals. A butterfly flutters past me with its brightly coloured wings. This, I know, started its life as an egg on a leaf. The egg changed into a caterpillar, the caterpillar into a chrysalis, the chrysalis into the butterfly. I have seen each of these stages take place. They amaze me.

I am amazed too when I see a new-born baby, with all its tiny features. I wonder even more when I think that this too started off as an egg, no bigger than a full stop.

I see things, of course, that arouse different feelings.

Animals hunt and kill other animals. Human beings become ill, grow old, and die. Earthquakes occur, volcanoes erupt, rivers flood. A country may be hit by a hurricane, another by drought. These all disturb me.

These observations and feelings lead me to ask two big questions.

The first is, is there anyone behind the universe? Is there someone who designed it and created it? The mechanisms that lead from a butterfly egg to an adult butterfly look as if they have been designed. Have they been?

I am aware that biologists explain the complexity of organisms like butterflies by the theory of evolution. According to this, complexity arises by a combination of random mutations in simpler organisms, and natural selection. If this is correct (and this has yet to be established for large-scale changes), then I wonder at the underlying constitution of the universe that allows such complexity to emerge. Is there someone behind *this*?

Whether the answer to this question is "Yes" or "No", it is a reasonable one to ask. When archaeologists discover an object that looks as if it might have been designed, they ask themselves whether a human being made it. Moreover, if they decide that the answer is "Yes", they do not then ask, "Who made the human being?" and start an infinite regress. I am taking their approach, and applying it to the universe.

The second question is, why is the universe as it is? Some of what I see inspires wonder, but some provokes horror. Why is the universe like this?

To seek answers to these questions, we turn first to modern science. This provides answers to many questions we ask. What does it have to say about these?

CHAPTER THREE

HELP FROM SCIENCE

Science cannot answer the question, is there anyone behind the universe? Scientists only make observations on the universe, and devise theories to relate these observations. They do not make observations outside the universe.

Science can, however, clarify the question to some extent, as I shall now explain. I shall do this for the general reader, avoiding technical language.

The scientific picture of the universe

Most scientists currently believe that the universe started 10–15 billion years ago as a speck of highly concentrated matter, which rapidly expanded (the "Big Bang"). From this expanding matter galaxies were formed, including the Milky Way.

Scientists believe that the earth was formed about 4,500 million years ago as a molten mass. As this cooled down, a crust developed. Today this consists of many distinct layers of rock (strata) one on top of the other. Examination of these layers shows that many of them have been formed by the accumulation and consolidation of sediment. Geologists believe that some of these were laid over a long period of time, but that others were deposited under more dramatic conditions, as would arise, for example, if a large meteorite struck the earth or a large volcano erupted.

Most scientists believe that life started on earth 3,500–3,800 million years ago by a process that involved the formation of increasingly complicated chemicals in lakes and seas, and the coming together of these to form simple organisms. The evidence for this is mainly circumstantial. Organisms are chemical systems. Components of these systems can be found in nature. The suggestion is that these components somehow came together to produce simple forms of life.

Most biologists believe that these forms then evolved into more complicated species, leading eventually to mammals and human beings. As I mentioned in the last chapter, they believe that this took place by a process involving mutations and natural selection. A mutation is an inheritable change in an organism's genes (the chemical sequences that determine an organism's characteristics). Mutants that are better equipped to survive and reproduce in a particular environment than unchanged members of a species gradually replace the latter in this environment.

To scientists, the various processes taking place in these developments are of two kinds. In one, the outcome is determined by laws. An example is the motion of the earth round the sun, and of the moon round the earth. These are determined by the laws of motion and gravity.

In processes of the second kind, outcomes are random. An example is radioactive decay. A sample of radioactive material contains a large number of potentially radioactive atoms. These decay randomly, leading to a gradual decrease in radioactivity, and not to a single burst, which is what would happen if they all decayed together. Most biologists believe that mutations occur randomly.

Note that some scientists disagree with the above account at certain points. For example, some cosmologists do not believe that the universe started in a big bang, but has always existed. Again, some physicists believe that processes that appear to be random are actually determined by laws, laws that have yet to be discovered. This was Einstein's conviction. I will mention other views where appropriate.

Implications of the scientific picture

At first sight, the two kinds of process scientists see in the universe have conflicting implications. Processes governed by laws imply that there is a designer; random processes imply that there is not.

The first implication is reinforced by the way in which the universe depends on the laws of nature. According to cosmologists, even a slight change in the laws would have produced a universe that is quite different from our own. They speak as if the laws have to be finely tuned to produce a universe in which human beings can exist (the so-called "anthropic principle").[1] Even if this turns out not to be the case, there is no doubt that the laws have to be exactly as they are for the universe to be exactly as it is.

To avoid the implications of this, some cosmologists postulate the existence of an infinite number of universes (a "multiverse"), with a random distribution of laws between them. This ensures the existence of our universe without the need for fine tuning.

However, randomness in nature does not necessarily imply lack of a designer. Randomness is required to give the universe the character it has. For example, gases are made up of microscopic particles moving randomly in all directions. If the particles all moved in the same direction, gases would have quite different properties. For example, if all the particles of the atmosphere moved from east to west, they would create a continual high wind that would make human life impossible. Biologists believe that random mutations provide a means by which organisms can adapt to major changes in their environment.

Moreover, randomness does not have to be undetermined. One way scientists simulate random processes is by using random numbers from a computer. These numbers, however, are produced by a quite definite mathematical procedure. To a mathematician or computer programmer, they are as determined as numbers obtained by any other mathematical procedure. A creator can therefore establish randomness in the universe as determinedly as the laws.

Similar considerations apply to single random events, e.g. a mutation that leads to a change in species. Scientists habitually ascribe these to "chance", in the sense that they have no immediate cause. This does not mean, however, that they have no ultimate cause. A creator of the universe would be capable of arranging such events if such events there be.

In conclusion, modern science points to there being a creator. It does not prove that there is, but it points to this. Even the idea that there are an infinite number of universes with a random distribution of laws between them does not avoid this conclusion, because these universes still have to be brought into being, and the random distribution established.

Furthermore, modern science points to there being a *single* creator. Science pictures the universe as being an integrated whole, running according to the same set of laws throughout. Such a universe requires someone to have complete control over its design and generation. The same is true of a multiverse, with each universe having to be an integrated whole, and the distribution of laws between them random.

The only alternative to a single creator is two or more creators acting in perfect harmony. While this is possible in principle, I will keep for the moment to a single creator.

If there is a creator, the question is, what is he or she like? The magnitude and complexity of the universe point to someone of great power and intellect. But what other qualities does he or she have? And what about all the things in nature that we shrink from? How do these fit into the picture?

CHAPTER FOUR

BEYOND SCIENCE

As human beings, we have no way of answering the questions, "What is the creator like?" and "Why is there suffering in the world?" All we can do is speculate. Philosophers try to do this, but come up with different answers. The only way we can know is if the creator somehow tells us.

But science seems to exclude this. Science pictures the universe as an isolated system, running on its own. There is no place for the involvement of a creator.

However, the scientific picture is only an approximation. Scientists have developed it by considering only the regular features of the universe. They omit all reports of events that appear to go against this regularity ("miracles"), however well attested these may be, and difficult to explain naturally. The scientific picture is thus, by its very nature, a partial one. It tells us how the universe functions most of the time, but does not tell us about any interventions the creator makes in it.

This point can be illustrated as follows. Imagine living alongside a railway line on which trains always run to time. By observing the times of trains over a period of time, you can work out the timetable for trains on the line. To do this, however, you have to omit a small number of observations that do not fit the general pattern. These correspond to special trains, and alterations to regular services made to accommodate them. The timetable you arrive at accordingly only describes what happens on the line most of the time, not all of the time.

Many reports of miracles are of course dubious. They are either poorly attested or can easily be explained naturally. There is therefore a temptation to dismiss the few that seem more genuine as being of the same kind.

We must remember, however, that the number of genuine miracles will depend on the relationship the creator wants with human beings. A large number would mean that he or she wanted to *force* us to take notice. A smaller number means that he or she wants us to be *free* whether to take notice or not. It means, in other words, that he or she wants us to take notice voluntarily, not coercively.

This puts us in the position of having to exercise *faith* that reports of these miracles are genuine, and that the creator has intervened in human history. Equally we have to exercise faith if we think that the reports are spurious. Either way we have to have faith.

What all this means is that, if we want answers to the questions we are asking, we have to be prepared to go beyond science, and consider claims that the creator has intervened in human history. We may reject these claims, but we are bound to consider them.

CHAPTER FIVE

POSSIBLE ANSWERS

The oldest religion in the world to believe in a single creator is Judaism. This later gave rise to Christianity, and later still, to Islam. All three religions believe that the creator (God) spoke miraculously to the founders of Judaism, especially Abraham, who lived somewhere between 2200 and 1800 BCE, and Moses, dated somewhere between 1600 and 1200 BCE.

These happenings are recorded in the first five books of the Jewish Bible (the books of Moses or Torah[1]). The standard Hebrew text of these was established by scholars between about 500 and 1000 CE, but agrees closely with fragments found among the Dead Sea Scrolls, dating from about the 1st century BCE, and with two earlier versions – a Greek translation made in the 3rd century BCE, and a Samaritan revision dating from about the 5th century BCE. In the 19th century scholars suggested that the books of Moses comprise four different versions of the early history of the Jews which were later combined into a single account by editors. However, the linguistic considerations on which this hypothesis is based are questionable.[2]

The Torah provides answers to the key questions we are asking. Whether we can accept these answers depends partly on their own credibility, and partly on whether we can believe the underlying claim that God spoke to the founders of Judaism. I will discuss the answers first, and then whether we can believe them.

The answers come in the first book of Moses (Genesis). This begins:[3]

In the beginning, God created the sky and the land [the universe].

The land was featureless and empty, darkness was over the face of the deep, and the Spirit of God hovered over the face of the waters.

Then God said, "Let there be light," and there was light. God saw that the light was good, and separated the light from the darkness. God called the light "day", and the darkness he called "night". There was evening and there was morning, one day.

Then God said, "Let there be a canopy in the middle of the waters, and let it separate waters from waters." So God made the canopy, and separated the waters that were under the canopy from the waters that were above the canopy, and it was so. God called the canopy "sky". There was evening and there was morning, a second day.

Then God said, "Let the waters under the sky be gathered in one place, and let the dry ground appear." And it was so. God called the dry ground "land", and the gathered waters he called "seas". And God saw that it was good.

Then God said, "Let the land sprout pasture, plants yielding seed, and fruit trees bearing fruit with their seed in it, according to their kinds, on the land." And it was so: the land brought forth pasture, plants yielding seed according to their kinds, and trees bearing fruit with their seed in it according to their kinds. And God saw that it was good. There was evening and there was morning, a third day.

Then God said, "Let there be lights in the canopy of the sky to separate the day from the night. Let them act as signs and mark seasons, days and years. Let them act as lights in the canopy of the sky to give light on the land." And it was so: God made the two great lights – the greater light to rule the day and the smaller light to rule the night – and the stars. God set them in the canopy of the sky to give light on the land, to rule over the day and over the night, and to separate the light from the darkness. And God saw that it was good. There was evening and there was morning, a fourth day.

Then God said, "Let the waters swarm with living organisms that swarm, and let birds fly about over the land, across the face of the canopy of the sky." So God created the great long-bodied water-creatures and every living organism that moves with which the waters swarm, according to their kinds, and every winged bird according to its kind. And God saw that it was good. Then God blessed them, saying, "Be fruitful and multiply, and fill the waters in the seas; and let the birds multiply on the land." There was evening and there was morning, a fifth day.

Then God said, "Let the land bring forth living organisms according to their kinds – livestock, creeping things, and wild animals according to their kinds." And it was so: God made the wild animals according to their kinds, the livestock according to their kinds, and all that creeps on the ground according to their kinds. And God saw that it was good.

Then God said [to his Spirit], "Let us make man in our image, after our likeness, and let them rule over the fish of the sea, over the birds of the sky, over the livestock, over all the land, and over all the creeping things that move on the land." So God created the [first] man in his image, in the image of God he created him, male and female he created them [amplified in 2:4–25: God made the man from "dust from the ground" and a woman from one of his ribs to become "one flesh" with him]. Then God blessed them, and said to them, "Be fruitful and multiply, and fill the land and subdue it. Rule over the fish of the sea, over the birds of the sky, and over every animal that moves on the land."

Then God said, "Take note, I have given you every plant yielding seed that is on the face of all the land, and every tree yielding seed in its fruit. You shall have this for food. And every wild animal, and every bird of the sky, and every living organism that creeps on the land, shall have all the greenery of plants for food." And it was so. Then God saw all that he had made, and, take note, *it was very good*. There was evening and there was morning, the sixth day.

Thus the sky and the land were finished, and all their array. So on the seventh day God had finished the work that he had done, and on that day *ceased* from all the work that he had done. So God blessed the seventh day and made it holy, because on it he ceased from all the work of creating that he had done.

(Genesis 1:1–2:3)

This account of creation is very different from other accounts from the ancient world, which are polytheistic and fanciful (see Box on next page). It is similar to the scientific account in making creation progressive, but differs from it in detail.

The differences between the Genesis account and the scientific one might lead us to dismiss Genesis as naive and mistaken. This, however, would be hasty. There are two possible ways of reconciling the accounts.[4]

First, the Genesis version could be partly figurative. This

Babylonian creation epic

This begins with Apsu, the god of fresh water, and Tiamat, the goddess of sea water, as all that exists. Apsu and Tiamat give birth to other gods. These make such a noise that Apsu decides to do away with them. They get to hear about this, and one of them, Ea, kills him. Tiamat is disturbed by this, and some of the gods, led by Kingu, induce her to seek revenge. Ea's son, Marduk, succeeds in overcoming her, splitting her in two. From her two parts he makes the sky and the earth, and creates stations in the sky for the gods (the stars, moon, and sun). To relieve the gods from menial tasks he creates mankind from the blood of Kingu. The gods thank him by building the city of Babylon and a temple to him there, and acclaim him as their king.[5]

---

would be to ensure that people in every age could understand it, and that faith in a scientific age is not pre-empted. If scientists could confirm Genesis, faith in a scientific age would be easier than in earlier ones.

Second, if the universe was created as described in Genesis, then on day 7 it would have been in a mature state. Stars would be shining (despite the time it takes for starlight to reach the earth), pebbles would be smooth, trees would have rings, and so on. The universe would accordingly have *appeared* to have had a history that it did not in reality have. To modern science, therefore, it would look very old, whereas in reality it would be very young.

However figurative or literal the Genesis passage may be, its underlying message is clear. *God* created the universe, and when he created it, everything in it was "very good". There was not the suffering that we see in the world now.

This leads the author to explain why there is now suffering in the world. He says that God made the first man and woman, put them in a garden, and told them that they could eat from every tree in the garden except "the tree of the knowledge of good and evil" (Genesis 2:4–25). He continues:

Now the snake was cleverer than all the other wild animals that YHWH God ["the Ruler God"][6] had made. He said to the woman, "Did God indeed say, 'You shall not eat from any tree in the garden'?"

The woman said to the snake, "We may eat of the fruit of the trees in the garden, but of the fruit of the tree that is in the middle of the garden, God said, 'You shall not eat of it, nor shall you touch it, lest you die.'"

The snake said to the woman, "You will not certainly die, for God knows that, on the day you eat of it, your eyes will be opened, and you will be like God, knowing good and evil."

The woman saw that the tree was good for food, and that it was pleasing to the eyes, and that it was desirable to make one wise. So she took of its fruit and ate. She also gave some to her husband who was with her, and he ate. Then the eyes of both of them were opened, and they knew that they were naked. So they sewed fig leaves together and made garments to go round themselves.

Then they heard the sound of YHWH God walking about in the garden in the cool breeze of the day. So the man and his wife hid themselves from the face of YHWH God among the trees of the garden. But YHWH God called to the man and said to him, "Where are you?"

He said, "I heard the sound of you in the garden, and I was afraid because I was naked, so I hid myself."

He said, "Who told you that you were naked? Have you eaten from the tree from which I commanded you not to eat?"

The man said, "The woman whom you gave to be with me, she gave me fruit from the tree, and I ate."

YHWH God said to the woman, "What is this you have done?"

The woman said, "The snake deceived me, and I ate."

Then YHWH God said to the snake, "Because you have done this, cursed are you above all livestock, and above all the other wild animals. On your belly you shall go, and you shall eat dust all the days of your life. I will put enmity between you and the woman, and between your offspring and her offspring. He will strike your head, and you will strike his heel."

To the woman he said, "I will greatly increase your toil and your pregnancies [to compensate for human beings dying]; in toil you shall bear children. Your desire will be to control your husband, but he will rule over you."

To the man he said, "Because you have listened to the voice of your wife, and have eaten from the tree about which I commanded you, saying, 'You shall not eat from it,' cursed is the ground because of you; in toil you shall eat from it all the days of your life. It shall bring forth thorns and thistles for you, and you shall eat the plants [not of the garden but] of the open country. By the sweat of your face you shall eat bread, until you return to the ground, for from it you were taken; for dust you are, and to dust you shall return.". . .

Then YHWH God said, "See, the man has become like one of us, knowing good and evil. Now we must act lest he reach out his hand, and take also from the tree of life, and eat and live for ever." Therefore YHWH God sent him out of the garden . . .

(Genesis 3:1–24)

Again, however we understand the details, the message is clear. Evil came into the world through creatures abusing the freedom God had given them. God allowed them to commit their crimes, and only intervened after they had done so. He then punished them for what they had done, and changed the natural order to make their lives less pleasant for them. In particular, he cursed the ground, and brought death on human beings.

The implication of this is that there was a major change in the workings of the universe at this point. The universe we now live in is "cursed", and is not as it was at the beginning. Science describes the workings of the cursed form, and its history back to the curse. Prior to this, scientific history relates to the history that the universe would have had if it had always been in a cursed state, not to its actual history.

Here then is an answer to the question, "Why is there suffering in the world?" Suffering is God's response to the disobedience of human beings from the beginning.

Can we believe this answer? We may feel that God's response is very harsh. But we have to be careful. God is God. We are not in a position to dictate what he is like.

Nevertheless, to accept this answer, we need to be convinced. We need therefore to look further into the Torah, which we shall do in the next chapter.

CHAPTER SIX

GUIDANCE FOR LIVING?

An implication of the opening chapters of Genesis is that God expects human beings to obey him, and if they do not, his punishment of them will be severe. The question then is, what does God want human beings to do and not do?

According to the Torah, God told Moses the answer to this after he had led the Jews out of slavery in Egypt. The resulting laws are set out in the second to fifth books of Moses (Exodus, Leviticus, Numbers, and Deuteronomy).

The foremost of these laws are the Ten Commandments. These were written on stone and placed in a box in a special sanctuary, at the centre of the nation's life. They are (abbreviated):

> I am YHWH your God . . . you shall have no other gods besides me.
>
> You shall not make for yourself a carved image, or any likeness of anything in the sky above, or on the land beneath, or in the

waters under the land; you shall not bow down to them or serve them . . .

You shall not use the name of YHWH your God emptily [frivolously or insincerely] . . .

Remember the Sabbath day [the day of cessation] so as to keep it holy. Six days you shall labour, and do all your work. The seventh day is a Sabbath [a day of cessation] for YHWH your God. You shall not do any work . . .

Honour your father and your mother . . .

You shall not murder.

You shall not commit adultery.

You shall not steal.

You shall not testify against your neighbour falsely.

You shall not covet . . . anything that belongs to your neighbour.

(Exodus 20:1–17)

In addition to these are a great many other laws relating to the worship of God and everyday life. There are also punishments for breaking these laws.

Do the laws of Moses support the claim that God spoke to the Jews through him? This is difficult to answer.

On the one hand, many of the laws are difficult to argue with. Though formulated negatively, their purpose is positive, the good of society. For example, the law against adultery protects marriage. Moses spoke of the laws as being "for good" (Deuteronomy 6:24, 10:12–13).

On the other hand, some laws are problematic. For example:

If anyone injures his neighbour, whatever he has done shall be done to him – fracture for fracture, eye for eye, tooth for tooth. Whatever injury he has given to someone shall be given to him.

(Leviticus 24:19–20)

This law was evidently designed to curb retaliation, and prevent escalation of conflicts. Even so, did God really tell Moses this?

Jesus

To answer this, we have to move on in the history of the Jews to another teacher, Jesus of Nazareth (*c.* 5 BCE – 30 CE).[1] Jews, Christians, and Muslims all believe that God also spoke through him. Christians believe more than this about him, but we shall restrict ourselves to his teaching for the moment.

There are four accounts of the life and teaching of Jesus that were accepted by early followers. Two are attributed to companions (Matthew and John), and two to followers who knew his companions (Mark and Luke). The oldest complete manuscript of these dates from the 4th century CE, but parts have been discovered dating from the 3rd century, and fragments from the 2nd.[2] The oldest is a few lines of John's account dated about 125 CE and kept in the John Rylands Library of the University of Manchester. There are also many later accounts of Jesus's life, some evidently written to modify his teaching or to discredit him.

In his teaching, Jesus raised the standard of the law of Moses. Addressing his followers in the "Sermon on the Mount", he said:

"You have heard that it was said to those of old, 'You shall not murder, and whoever murders shall be subject to judgment.' But I say to you that everyone who is angry with his brother shall be subject to judgment . . .

"You have heard that it was said, 'You shall not commit adultery.' But I say to you that everyone who looks at a woman lustfully has already committed adultery with her in his heart . . .

"It was also said, 'Whoever divorces his wife, let him give her a certificate of severence.' But I say to you that everyone who divorces his wife, except on account of fornication [premarital infidelity],[3] makes her commit adultery . . .

"Again you have heard that it was said to those of old, 'You shall not make oaths falsely, but carry out your oaths to the Ruler [YHWH].' But I say to you, do not swear at all . . .

"You have heard that it was said, 'An eye for an eye and a tooth for a tooth.' But I say to you, do not resist evil. Rather, if anyone strikes you on your right cheek, turn to him the other also . . .

"You have heard that it was said, 'You shall seek the good of your neighbour and ill of your enemy.'[4] But I say to you, seek the good of your enemies . . ."

(Matthew 5:21–48)

Jesus went on to set high standards in other areas of life, and to call upon his followers to keep these standards.

On another occasion, Jesus explained why Moses had set a lower standard than he did:

Some Pharisees [members of a strict Jewish sect] came up to him and tested him, saying, "Is it lawful to divorce one's wife for any cause?"

He answered, "Have you not read that from the beginning the Creator made them male and female, and said, 'Because of this, a man shall leave his father and mother, and shall cleave to his wife, and the two shall become one flesh'? So they are no longer two, but one flesh. What then God has joined together, let a human being not separate."

> They said to him, "Why then did Moses command one to give her a certificate of severance, and divorce her?"
>
> He said to them, "Moses allowed you to divorce your wives because of your hardness of heart, but from the beginning this has not been the way. And I say to you that whoever divorces his wife, except for fornication, and marries another, commits adultery."
>
> (Matthew 19:3–9)

Jesus explains here that Moses had set a lower standard because many people are not capable of keeping to a higher one. He accordingly allowed divorce, but sought to regulate it. Jesus's answer explains why God sometimes tolerated lower standards of conduct in Jewish history than we might have expected, as recorded in the Jewish Bible.

Jesus's followers responded to his teaching on divorce by expressing concern about its strictness. He replied that his high standard is not for everyone. Some can keep it naturally, some can be made to do so by human pressure, but some also can make themselves keep it, for the sake of being under God's rule (Matthew 19:10–12).[5] I shall return to this in the next chapter.

On one further occasion, Jesus questioned the fitness of people to carry out some of the punishments in the law of Moses:[6]

> At dawn he came again to the temple . . . The scribes and the Pharisees brought a woman who had been caught in adultery, and, standing her in the middle, they said to him, "Teacher, this woman has been caught in the act of adultery. Now in the Law, Moses commanded us to stone such women. What then do you say? They said this to test him, so that they might have grounds

to accuse him [either of going against Moses or against the Romans, who did not allow Jews to carry out executions].

But Jesus bent down and wrote with his finger on the ground. But as they continued to ask him, he stood up and said to them, "He who is sinless among you, let him be the first to throw a stone at her."

Again he bent down and wrote on the ground. Then those who heard went away one by one, beginning with the older ones, and he was left alone, with the woman still in the middle.

Jesus stood up and said to her, "Woman, where are they? Has no one condemned you?"

She said, "No one, sir."

Jesus said, "Neither do I condemn you. Go, from now on sin no more."

(John 8:2–11)

Jesus does not question here the seriousness of the woman's wrongdoing. On another occasion he described adultery as "evil" (Mark 7:20–23). What he is questioning is the fitness of people to carry out capital punishment for such a wrongdoing.

The teaching of Jesus makes it easier to accept the claim that God spoke through Moses. It also supports the claim that God spoke through him. We shall return to this in the next chapter.

Jesus's standards are higher, not only than Moses', but also in many respects than Muhammad's (c. 570–632 CE). For example, Muhammad permitted divorce,[7] and taught his followers to fight their enemies.[8] Although he commended Jesus, he seems not to have been fully aware of his teaching. This may be the fault of Christians, who in every age have not followed the teaching of Jesus very well.

CHAPTER SEVEN

HELP FOR LIVING

The high standards Jesus set in his teaching raise two pressing questions. The first is, how can we possibly keep these standards? We can keep some by our own efforts, depending on our make-up (different people can keep different ones). But what about the standards we cannot keep by our own efforts? How can we achieve these?

And what about the standards we fail to keep? If God punishes disobedience, will he not punish us? Even if he excuses us for failing to keep the standards that we are unable to keep, what about the standards we could have kept and have not?

These questions were answered by Jewish prophets in a period when the Jewish nation went into decline, and was conquered by its neighbours (8–6th century BCE). They foresaw a day when God would forgive his people for their sins, and help them to keep his standards. The prophet Jeremiah wrote:

"Take note, the days are coming," says YHWH, "when I will make a new covenant with [the nation of Israel]. It will not be like the covenant that I made with their fathers on the day when I took them by the hand to bring them out of the land of Egypt, my covenant that they broke, though I was a husband to them," says YHWH. "But this is the covenant that I will make with [the nation] after those days," says YHWH, "I will put my law inside them, and write it on their hearts. I will be their God, and they shall be my people. No longer shall one have to teach another, saying, 'Know YHWH,' for they shall all know me, from the least of them to the greatest," says YHWH. "For I will forgive their iniquity, and remember their sin no more."

(Jeremiah 31:31–34)

Likewise Ezekiel wrote:

"[Thus says the Ruler YHWH:] I will take you from the nations, and gather you out of all the lands, and bring you to your own terrain. I will sprinkle clean water on you, and you shall be clean: from all your filth and all your idols, I will cleanse you. I will give you a new heart, and put a new spirit within you: I will remove the heart of stone from your flesh, give you a heart of flesh, put my Spirit within you, and enable you to follow my rules, and practise my judgments."

(Ezekiel 36:24–27)

Here God promises supernatural help to keep his laws, the help of his "Spirit".

Further, the prophets foresaw that God would do these things through a person, the Messiah. Isaiah wrote:

The people who walk in darkness [in the prophet's vision of the future] have seen a great light; those who live in a land of deep shadow, on them has light shined. . . .

For to us a child is born, to us a son is given; and the government shall be on his shoulder, and his name shall be called Wonderful Counsellor, Mighty God, Everlasting Father, Prince of Peace. Of the increase of his government and of peace there shall be no end, on the throne of [esteemed king] David and over his kingdom, to establish it and to uphold it, with justice and righteousness, from this time on and for ever. The zeal of omnipotent YHWH will do this.

(Isaiah 9:2, 6–7)

Isaiah also foresaw that the Messiah would come, not just for Jews, but for all people:

See my servant, whom I uphold, my chosen, in whom my being delights. I have put my Spirit on him; he shall bring justice to the nations. He shall not cry out or lift up his voice, or make it heard in the street. A crushed reed he shall not break, and a dimly-burning wick he shall not extinguish. He shall execute justice according to truth. *He* shall not burn dimly or be crushed until he has established justice in the land. The lands too along the coast and across the seas will wait for his law.

Thus says God YHWH . . ., "I YHWH have called you in righteousness. I will hold your hand, keep you, and give you as a covenant to the people, and a light to the nations: to open blind eyes and to release prisoners from prison – yes, those who sit in darkness from where they are being held. I am YHWH; that is my name. My glory I will not give to another, nor my praise to carved images. Take note, the former things [I foretold] have come to pass, and I announce new things: before they appear you hear of them."

(Isaiah 42:1–9)

Isaiah went on to describe how the Messiah would secure forgiveness of sins:

Who has believed what we have heard? To whom is the "arm" of YHWH [his servant] revealed? For he grew up before him like a baby still being suckled, or a root sprouting out of dry ground [i.e. he was very weak]. He had no stature or majesty that we should notice him, no appearance that we should be drawn towards him. He was despised and forsaken by people, a man with pains and suffering illnesses.[1] Like one from whom people hide their faces, he was despised, and we put him out of our thoughts. But in fact he has borne *our* illnesses and carried *our* pains. Yet we thought he was being stricken [punished], smitten by God and humbled. But he was pierced for *our* transgressions; he was bruised for *our* iniquities. The chastisement required to bring *us* peace was on him, and by his wounds we are healed. All we like sheep have gone astray, we have all turned to our own way; and YHWH has laid on him the iniquity of us all.

(Isaiah 53:1–6)

This would not however be the end:

Yet it pleased YHWH to bruise him, to make him ill. For if he gives his life to atone for sin, he shall see offspring, prolong his days, and the pleasure of YHWH shall prosper in his hand. He shall see [the fruit] of the travail in his life, and be satisfied. "Through his knowledge [of my ways] my righteous servant shall secure righteousness for many, and bear their iniquities. Therefore I will give him a share with the many, and he shall share spoil with a great number, because he poured out his life to death, and was numbered with transgressors. He indeed bore the sin of many, and interceded for the transgressors."

(Isaiah 53:10–12)

Fulfilment?

Jesus gave strong indications that he saw himself as having come to fulfil these prophecies, and Christians believe that he did. In particular, they believe that he allowed himself to be put to death to secure forgiveness of sins, that he rose from the dead, that he was then taken up to God, and that he now provides supernatural help to those who want to keep his standards. They accordingly refer to him as "Christ" (Greek for Messiah).

These are big claims. Both Jews and Muslims reject them. On what grounds might we accept them?

The claim that Jesus was put to death, though rejected by Muslims,[2] is supported by the Roman historian, Tacitus. He states that: "Christ . . . was executed in the reign of Tiberius through procurator Pontius Pilate" (*Annals* 15.44).

Pontius Pilate was governor of Judaea (the region around Jerusalem) from 26 to 36 CE. Tacitus does not specify the method of execution, but according to Jesus's followers, this was by crucifixion, i.e. by being nailed to a wooden cross and lifted up to die. A soldier made sure that he was dead by thrusting a spear into his side.

The key claim is that Jesus rose from the dead. His companions reported that, on the third day after his death, they found the stone in front of his tomb rolled away, and only his grave-clothes inside. They further reported that, later that day, he appeared to them in bodily form, and continued to do so over a period of 40 days, until he was taken up from them.

The question is, can we believe these reports? This depends very much on the credibility of the witnesses. Were they being honest, or did they make up the story for their own purposes? If they were being honest, were they mistaken? Did someone take Jesus's body from the grave, and did his companions have experiences that led them to imagine that Jesus had risen?

The question of whether Jesus's companions were being honest can be answered with some certainty. There are strong indications that they were. In the first place, many people accepted their testimony and Christianity spread. This is significant because they were at the same time teaching Jesus's high standards for living. People would hardly have been impressed if his companions had not tried to live up to these standards, and always tell the truth.

Secondly, Jesus's companions were prepared to give their testimony in the face of severe persecution. Many lost their lives in the process. This implies that they believed what they were saying.

Thirdly, his companions were very honest in reporting their own failings. For example, they admitted that they had twice had an argument about which of them was the greatest (Luke 9:46-48, 22:24–27). They also confessed that, on the night before Jesus's death, when he asked them to stay awake and pray, they fell asleep (Luke 22:39–46). A willingness to admit failings is a good sign of honesty.

But were Jesus's companions mistaken? From what they tell us, they did not think they were. Matthew explains why they were sure that nobody had taken Jesus's body from the tomb. He says that the Jewish authorities persuaded Pontius Pilate to place a guard on the tomb to prevent Jesus's body from being stolen (27:62–66). When the tomb was found to be empty, the authorities then bribed the guards to say that his followers had stolen his body while they were asleep (28:11–15).

Furthermore, Jesus's companions admitted that they *did* initially have doubts about the resurrection. Luke reports what happened when Jesus appeared to a gathering of them on the first day:

[While they were still talking], he himself stood among them, and said to them, "Peace to you!"

But they became alarmed and afraid, thinking that they were seeing a spirit. So he said to them, "Why are you troubled, and why do questions arise in your hearts? See my hands and my feet, that it is I myself. Touch me and see, because a spirit does not have flesh and bones as you see that I have." And when he had said this he showed them his hands and his feet.

While they still did not believe for joy and wondered, he said to them, "Have you any food here?" And they gave him a piece of cooked fish, and he took it and ate before them.

Then he said to them, "This is the meaning of my words, which I spoke to you while I was still with you, that everything written about me in [the Jewish Bible] must be fulfilled."

(Luke 24:36–44)

John adds:

Now Thomas . . . was not with them when Jesus came. So the other disciples said to him, "We have seen the Ruler."

But he said to them, "Unless I see in his hands the mark of the nails, and put my finger into where the nails were, and put my hand into [the spear-wound in] his side, I will never believe."

Eight days later his disciples were inside again, and Thomas was with them. Although the doors were locked, Jesus came and stood in the middle and said, "Peace to you!"

Then he said to Thomas, "Bring your finger here, and see my hands; and bring your hand, and put it into my side. Do not be unbelieving but believing."

Thomas answered him, "My Ruler and my God!"

Jesus said to him, "You have believed because you have seen me. Blessed are those who have not seen and yet have believed."

(John 20:24–29)

Note that the disciples refer to Jesus here as "Ruler" (Greek *Kurios*). This word was used of the Roman emperor, and to represent YHWH in the Greek translation of the Talmud.[3]

A further test

A subjective test is possible of the claim that we can receive supernatural help to keep Jesus's standards. This is to make the response that he had instructed his companions to call for.

We can find details of this in the accounts of his life, and also in the "Acts of the Apostles", a book on the lives of his companions following his death. This describes how one of them (Peter) spoke to a large crowd in Jerusalem about the death and resurrection of Jesus. When they asked how they should respond, he told them:

"Repent, and be baptized, every one of you, in the name of Jesus Christ for the forgiveness of your sins, and you shall receive the gift of the Holy Spirit."

(Acts 2:38)

Here "repent" means "change from the way you have been living to the way God wants you to live". This entails committing oneself to keep Jesus's standards.

Being "baptized in the name of Jesus Christ for the forgiveness of sins" means undergoing immersion in water while his name is being said. Immersion in water symbolizes the washing away of sins, and an end to one's old way of life and start of a new one. (Many people become Christians simply by praying to Jesus for forgiveness, but baptism is the way he appointed.)

Finally, the "gift of the Holy Spirit" is the gift of supernatural help to follow Jesus, and to serve him in the world. In particular, it is the provision of help to keep Jesus's standards beyond our own ability to do so.

If then we sincerely follow this course, we should receive such help to keep his standards. If we do, we have confirmation of Jesus's claims. Christians speak of experiencing the risen Jesus and the Holy Spirit in other ways, but the authenticity of these is less clear-cut than the ability to keep a standard that we know that we could not keep ourselves.

CHAPTER EIGHT

FURTHER TEACHING

We have seen that Jesus taught high moral standards, and promised forgiveness of sins and help to keep his standards. Here I sketch some of his other teaching. (I have had to be very selective.)

Purpose of life

In the Sermon on the Mount, Jesus told his followers:

> "*You* are the salt of the earth. But if the salt has lost its potency, with what shall it be made salty? It remains good for nothing, except to be thrown out and trodden down by people.
>
> "*You* are the light of the world. A city set on a hill cannot be hidden. Nor do people light a lamp and put it under a tub, but on a lamp-stand, and it gives light to all in the house. In the same way, let your light shine before people, so that they may see your good deeds, and praise your Father in heaven."

(Matthew 5:13–16)

Jesus here gives his followers the task of being "salt" and "light" to society. The main use of salt at the time was to preserve meat and fish from going rotten. Light enables people on a dark night to see where to go, and to avoid stumbling over things. Jesus is saying, "You are to live in such a way as to help people to see the right way to live, and prevent society from degenerating."

When Jesus says, "Let people see your good deeds", he excludes deeds like helping the poor, praying, and fasting. He said that these should be done discreetly (Matthew 6:1–18).

Note that Jesus refers here to God as "Father", and his dwelling place as "heaven". The word for the latter is the same as that used for "sky". The picture is of God dwelling in the sky above the stars (Deuteronomy 26:15).

Concern for others

On one occasion, a lawyer asked Jesus, "Which is the great commandment in the Law [sc. of Moses]?" Jesus replied,

> "'You shall seek the good of the Ruler your God [i.e. his honour] with all your heart and with all your life and with all your mind.' This is the great and first commandment. The second is like it: 'You shall seek the good of your neighbour as of yourself.' On these two commandments hang all the Law and the Prophets."
> (Matthew 22:34–40)

The word I have translated "seek the good of" (Greek *agapaō*) is usually rendered "love". The word does not mean, however, that we have to have a warm feeling towards another, but a practical concern for his or her honour and welfare.

This comes out in the answer Jesus gave when another lawyer asked, "And who is my neighbour?" (Luke 10:25–37). Jesus told him a parable (he often used parables).

This concerned a man who had been robbed and beaten up. A priest saw the man but did not help him. A temple-worker also saw the man and did not help him. Then a hated foreigner (a Samaritan) saw him, and he *did* help him. He attended to his wounds, and paid for him to be looked after until he recovered. This makes clear what "neighbour" means, and also *agapaō*.

Note that Jesus is *summarizing* the Law in the word *agapaō*, not replacing it. An act is not loving if it breaks the Law (1 John 5:2).

Men and women

We do not have a record of Jesus's teaching on gender. The nearest we have comes in his answer to another question (Luke 20:27–40). In this he says that, while in this life, men and women have different roles (v. 34), in the life to come, they will have the same (vv. 35–36). Consistent with this, he appointed only men to be leaders (Luke 6:12–16), but included women in his team (Luke 8:1–3), and revealed himself to them first after his resurrection (Matthew 28:1–10).[1]

As we saw in Chapter 6, Jesus taught that men and women should marry, and that marriage should be for life (Matthew 19:3–9). He also implied that, if they do not marry, they should remain celibate (cf. vv. 11–12) – he described sexual activity outside marriage as "evil" (Mark 7:20–23).[2]

Children

The value Jesus placed on children comes out in the following incident:

Then little children were brought to him that he might put his hands on them and pray. But the disciples rebuked those who brought them. But Jesus said, "Let the little children come to me and do not impede them, for the rule of heaven is for such as these." And he put his hands on them and went away.

(Matthew 19:13–15)

Money

Jesus had much to say about money and possessions. This is summed up in his call to his followers:

"Do not be anxious about your life, what you will eat, nor about your body, what you will wear, . . . for the nations of the world seek after all these things, and your Father knows that you need them. Seek rather his rule, and these things shall be added to you.

"Fear not, little flock, your Father has been pleased to give you [the blessings of] his rule. Sell your possessions and give to the poor: provide for yourselves purses that do not wear out, a treasure in heaven that does not fail, where no thief comes near and no moth destroys. For where your treasure is, there your heart will be also."

(Luke 12:22–34)

I hardly need say that this is very challenging.

Life as a follower

Jesus warned his followers, "in the world you will have tribulation" (John 16:33). His early followers did indeed have tribulation – they suffered persecution, sickness, poverty, and other hardships. But he promised that he would be *with* them in their tribulation: "I will not leave you on your own: I will come to you" (John 14:18). From the context, he is referring here to being with them as a spirit, as God is a spirit.

Prayer

In the Sermon on the Mount, Jesus taught his followers to pray along the following lines:

> "Our Father in heaven,
> may your name be revered,
> your rule come,
> your will be done,
> on earth as it is in heaven.
> Give us today our daily bread.
> And forgive us our debts [failings and wrongdoings],
> as we forgive our debtors.
> And lead us not into testing,
> but rescue us from evil."

(Matthew 6:9–13)

This prayer contains six petitions. Of these, the first three express the desire that what *God* wants to happen will happen. Only the second three are requests for ourselves.

In the petition, "Forgive us our debts", the word "debt" suggests a failure to do what is right. Jesus made it clear, however, that "debt" also includes doing what is wrong (Matthew 6:14–15, Luke 11:2–4).

In the last petition, Jesus refers to (lit.) "the evil". He spoke elsewhere of "the Devil" and "Satan". He was evidently aware of an influence in the universe acting against the good of human beings. The Christian Bible traces this back to the anarchy in the garden described in Genesis 3 (Revelation 12:9, 20:2).

Death for followers

On the night before his own death, Jesus assured his followers:

> "Let not your hearts be troubled. You believe in God; believe also in me. In my Father's household there are many places to live. If it were not so, would I have told you that I go to prepare a place for you? And if I go and prepare a place for you, I will come back and take you to myself, that where I am you may be also."
>
> (John 14:1–3)

Here Jesus promises to take his followers to be with him in heaven. Their bodies will die, but their personalities will live on.

This is possible because personality resides in *patterns* among cells in the brain. These patterns can persist after death in the thinking organ of a spiritual being.

The Great Commission

After his resurrection, Jesus gave his companions the task of telling others about him:

> "All authority in heaven and on earth has been given to me. Go then and make disciples of all nations, baptizing them in the name of the Father and of the Son and of the Holy Spirit, and teaching them to observe all that I have commanded you. And see, I am with you always, to the end of the age."
>
> (Matthew 28:18–20).

The early Christians took this to be a task that they were all called to share in, with those who had a particular ability to tell others about Jesus being sent out and supported.

Note that Jesus speaks here of having been given "all authority in heaven and on earth". This implies that God now rules the universe through him. I discuss the triple name ("Father, Son, and Holy Spirit") below.

Note also the focus on the *teaching* of Jesus: "Go then and make disciples of all nations . . . teaching them to observe all that I have commanded you." The word "disciple" literally means "learner".

Future of the world

Jesus told his followers that he would one day come back to the world to reclaim it for himself and for them. He linked this with the prophecy of Isaiah that there will one day be "a new heaven and a new earth", with the curse described in Genesis removed (Isaiah 65:17–25, Matthew 19:28). He said that there will be increased tribulation first. Then he would come in the manner the prophets had foreseen (Isaiah 13:10, 34:4; Daniel 7:13–14):

> "Immediately after the tribulation of those days, the sun shall be darkened, the moon shall not give its light, the stars shall fall from the sky, and the powers of heaven shall be shaken. Then the sign of the Son of Humanity shall appear in the sky, and all the peoples of the earth will beat themselves. They will see the Son of Humanity coming on the clouds of the sky with power and great glory. And he shall send his angels with a loud trumpet call, and they shall gather his chosen from the four winds, from one end of heaven to the other."
>
> (Matthew 24:29–31)

When this happens, Jesus will deal with all the evil in the world, and establish a regime of righteousness and peace. He will also give his followers new bodies for life on the new earth. He will make these by resurrecting and changing their old bodies. (I am distilling the teaching of the Bible here.)

Further details

More about the Christian faith can be found in the Christian Bible. This is in two parts, the Old Testament and the New Testament. The Old Testament comprises the books of Moses and other Jewish books written before Jesus came. The New Testament comprises the four accounts of the life and teaching of Jesus I have been quoting from, the Acts of the Apostles, and letters written by leading followers to various groups of Christians.

As we have seen, one of the accounts of Jesus's life was written by Luke. He was a physician, who set out to bring together what was known about Jesus (Luke 1:1–4). He also wrote the Acts of the Apostles. His two books provide a suitable introduction for the general reader.

Human or divine?

The life of Jesus raises some difficult questions. In much of what he did and said, he was very human. Thus, he prayed to God, addressing him in the same way as he taught his followers to address him ("Father"). He made it clear that the miracles he performed were not wrought by him, but by the Spirit of God. He frequently referred to himself as "the Son of Humanity".

Sometimes, however, he acted in a way that we would expect only God to act. Thus, he pronounced forgiveness of sins. He promised his followers that, after his death and resurrection, he would send God's Spirit to help them. He spoke of having lived "before the world began" (John 17:5).

The picture is of someone who is both human and divine. But how can someone be both human and divine? And if Jesus was divine, how can there only be one God?

Attempts were made in the early centuries of Christianity to avoid these questions by asserting that Jesus was *not* both human and divine. Christian leaders, however, resisted these attempts in a series of meetings called for this purpose (Councils). These questions, therefore, remain.

The way the Christian Bible answers these questions is as follows. God, before he made the universe, "begat" a Son – someone who was both part of him and distinct from him. Then, at the appointed time, the Son became human. He emptied himself of his divine powers, and allowed himself to be born of a virgin, trusting that his Father would help him in his humanity. After his death and resurrection, he returned to being "Son of God" in heaven.

Key passages in the Bible explaining this are as follows. The first comes at the beginning of John's account of the life of Jesus:

In the beginning was the Word [the Speaker], and the Word was with God, and the Word was God. He was with God in the beginning. All things were made through him, and without him was not anything made that was made. . . .

And the Word became flesh [human] and dwelt among us, and we have seen his glory, the glory as of the only begotten [the only Son] from the Father, full of grace and truth. . . .

> No one has ever seen God; the only begotten God [the Son], who is close to the Father, he has made him known.
>
> (John 1:1–3, 14, 18)

The second passage is from a letter written by Paul, who led the early Christians in taking the message of Jesus to non-Jews (Gentiles):

> Have this attitude [of humility] among yourselves, which was also in Christ Jesus, who, though being in the form of God, did not deem equality with God something to be clung on to, but emptied himself, taking the form of a slave, becoming like human beings. And having come to be like a human being in appearance, he humbled himself, becoming obedient even to death, even death on a cross. Therefore God indeed highly exalted him, and bestowed on him the name that is above every name, so that at the name of Jesus every knee should bow, in heaven and on earth and under the earth, and every tongue acknowledge that Jesus Christ is Ruler, to the glory of God the Father.
>
> (Philippians 2:5–11)

Thus we can say that Jesus was God's Son in human form, and that the Son and the Father, though distinct, are one. The Holy Spirit is also distinct, but one with the Father and the Son. Jesus referred to the Holy Spirit as "the finger of God" (compare Luke 11:20 with Matthew 12:28).

We can now understand the triple name to be pronounced at baptism, "Father, Son, and Holy Spirit". The "Son" refers to Jesus.

CHAPTER NINE

VARIATIONS

Primitive Christianity

The life and teaching of Jesus gave rise to primitive Christianity. This was spread by his followers, led by men he selected for this purpose ("apostles"). Luke describes how this spread took place in the Acts of the Apostles. A group of Christians meeting together was called (in Greek) an *ekklēsia* ("church").

The apostles were also responsible for regulating belief and practice. They did this by visiting churches and writing letters. They also held a meeting in Jerusalem to decide how far Gentile Christians had to adopt Jewish customs and practices. Their answer was: only so far as to avoid offending Jewish sensibilities.

Christians met in houses or halls. They did so on the first day of the week (Sunday) because this was the day on which Jesus rose from the dead. They sang hymns, prayed, received instruction, and gave money to help the poor. They also did what Jesus had requested, and re-enacted the last supper he had with his followers.

Local congregations were led by men called *episkopoi* ("overseers") or *presbuteroi* ("elders"). These were appointed for their leadership qualities and integrity. Also appointed were *diakonoi* ("deacons" and "deaconesses"). These attended to practical needs of members of the congregation.

Later Christianity

Christianity began during the Roman Empire. For two and a half centuries, emperors opposed it. Some of the first Christians suffered severe persecution at their hands.

All this was changed by the emperor Constantine, who issued an edict in 313 CE granting freedom of worship to Christians. This led to the building of Christian places of worship and the incorporation of Christianity into the state.

In later centuries, tensions developed between the church in Rome and the church in Constantinople. This led to schism between them in 1054 CE. Since then the Roman Catholic Church and Eastern Orthodox Churches have functioned independently.

In the 16th century some priests in the Roman Catholic Church were telling people that they could avoid God's punishment for sins by paying money to the Church. Concern about this led to the Reformation, and the establishment of new churches that sought to get back to the teaching of the Bible. These churches took many forms. In England, Thomas Cranmer and others reformed the Church of England, which Henry VIII had severed from Rome.

Since the Reformation there have been many new movements within reformed churches, leading to a wide variety of different kinds today. Pentecostals, for example, emphasize spiritual experiences, and the Salvation Army, social action. Other movements within Christianity have led to the formation of sects like the Mormons and Jehovah's Witnesses.

Christianity today

Because of this history, Christianity today varies widely in belief and practice. Readers who visit churches will find big differences between them.

Some of these differences are unimportant. People vary in temperament and background. Jesus did not lay down detailed rules for church life, and the apostles allowed some variation in belief and practice (e.g. over the eating of meat). Even so, a good church will cater for different kinds of people, and make its services as inclusive as possible.

Other differences between churches are more deep-seated, and involve departures from early Christian teaching. Churches justify these departures on various grounds. Some invoke *tradition* (e.g. in restricting the leadership of churches to celibate men). Some invoke *reason* (e.g. in saying that the resurrection did not literally happen, but was the way Jesus's followers explained their experiences after his death). Some invoke changes in *culture* (e.g. in allowing women to lead churches). Some invoke *feelings* (e.g. to decide what is right). Sects rely on their own interpretation of the Bible, or further revelation (e.g. to Joseph Smith in the case of the Mormons).

Each of these justifications has its dangers. In the case of tradition, there is the problem that tradition does not make something right. For example, some of the apostles were married. Restricting leadership to celibate men goes against this precedent, however many years it has been practised.

The problem with reason is that a reasoned argument is only as good as the presuppositions on which it is based. For example, if we presuppose that nature is autonomous, we conclude that the resurrection did not literally happen. But is nature autonomous? There is no reason why it should be.

Invoking culture presupposes that Jesus and his apostles were bound by culture, and that their teaching was relative. But were they so bound? In many ways they went against contemporary culture. For example, they went against Jewish culture in not requiring Christians to live as Jews, and against Graeco-Roman culture in outlawing pagan practices. Their teaching on divorce (Chapter 6) went against *both* cultures. In their treatment of women, they broke with Jewish culture in having them as co-workers, and with Greek culture in not appointing them as priestesses.[1]

The problem with relying on feelings is that it is very difficult to distinguish between a genuine spiritual feeling and a spurious one. We have the feeling, but does it come from God or our own psyche? The apostles called on Christians to "test the spirits" (1 John 4:1).

Finally, Jesus did not say that someone would come after the apostles to speak for him. Rather, he said that there would be "false Christs and false prophets", and told his followers to watch out for them (Matthew 24:4–5, 10–11, 23–25).

My conclusion from this is that the best churches are those that seek to follow the teaching of Jesus and his apostles as closely as possible. Jesus gave the clear impression that his teaching was for all time. He said:

"Sky and earth shall pass away, but my words shall never pass away."

(Matthew 24:35)

The traditional name for churches that follow the teaching of Jesus and his apostles closely is "Evangelical" (from *euaggelion*, "good news"). However, many contemporary Evangelical churches fail to do this. They follow some parts of the New Testament, but neglect other parts. Churches that do follow the New Testament closely are better described as "Scriptural".

In practice, within the many divisions of Christendom, there are individual churches that, to some degree at least, seek to base their beliefs and practices on the New Testament. While some of their customs may reflect their particular history and affiliation, their main aim nevertheless is to encourage their members to live as Jesus taught. Most readers should be able to find such a church near to where they live.

A serious charge

A charge that can be levelled against Christianity is that Christians have done some terrible things in the world. One only has to think of the Crusades sent from Rome in the Middle Ages to wrest the Holy Land from Muslims. These were shameful.

However, there is nothing in the teaching of Jesus to encourage these activities. The opposite is the case as we have seen. Those who have done these things have either misunderstood his teaching, or chosen to disregard it.

There are happily many examples of Christians who have done good things in the world, like the great social reformers in the 19th century, William Wilberforce, Elizabeth Fry, Lord Shaftesbury, and others. Wilberforce campaigned to abolish slavery, Elizabeth Fry to improve conditions in prisons, and Lord Shaftesbury to end child labour.

Many of the early scientists were Christians. Michael Faraday, who was a director of the Royal Institution, and whose researches led to the generation and use of electricity, was also an elder of a small, Bible-based church.

There have also been many ordinary Christians who, at various times and in different places, lived in a way that made society better than it might otherwise have been. This has been acknowledged by secular writers. For example, the French historian, Elie Halévy, wrote:[2]

> . . . during the nineteenth century Evangelical [Scriptural] religion was the moral cement of English society. It was the influence of the Evangelicals which invested the British aristocracy with an almost stoic [austere] dignity, restrained the plutocrats who had newly risen from the masses from vulgar ostentation and debauchery, and placed over the proletariate a select body of workmen enamoured of virtue and capable of self-restraint.

Few will dispute that the secularization of Britain in the 20th century has been accompanied by increased levels of family breakdown, crime, and antisocial behaviour. Karl Marx famously said that "religion is the opium of the people". Alas for many in Britain today the reverse is the case.

CHAPTER TEN

CONCLUSION

Our quest for truth to live by has led us to Jesus of Nazareth. We have had to take steps of faith, but these are no bigger than on paths that lead to other conclusions. Much rests on the life and teaching of Jesus himself, about which readers can find more in the Christian Bible.

We now have answers to the questions I posed in the Introduction. John and Sally are having an affair. Is there a truth to guide them in this situation? The answer is, "Yes". They are committing adultery and should stop.

Peter is despairing. Is there a truth for him? The answer again is "Yes". Difficult though his situation is, he can have a purpose in life, to be salt and light in the world, and to serve the risen Christ.

So how should we respond? Jesus tells us in one of his parables:

"Again, the rule of heaven is like a merchant seeking fine pearls, who, on finding one of great value, went away and sold all that he had and bought it."

(Matthew 13:45–46)

Proceeding further

Readers who would like to proceed further can find out more about the Christian faith by reading the Bible and attending a local church. A suitable place to start reading the Bible is Luke (see page 48), and a suitable church is one that seeks to follow the Bible closely (see pages 53–55). Many such churches provide courses for those who want to learn about the Christian faith.

Readers can also start praying and amending their lives. They can pray for forgiveness for past failures and for help to live rightly. They can also start using the prayer Jesus taught ("the Lord's Prayer", page 45). The appropriate next step then is to ask to be baptized (see pages 39–40).

I wish readers well if they proceed in this way.

NOTES

Chapter 1: Introduction

1. A scientific theory can never be completely certain because it may fail to explain observations that have not yet been made. Note, however, that a theory that does fail to explain a new observation may not be completely wrong, but an approximation to a better theory, and still valid under certain conditions.

Chapter 3: Help from science

1. See, e.g., Paul Davies, *The Goldilocks Enigma*, Allen Lane, London, 2006.

Chapter 5: Possible answers

1. Hebrew *tōrāh*, "instruction".

2. See, e.g., Derek Kidner, *Genesis*, Tyndale, London, 1967, pp. 16–22, 97–100, 184–186, 200–203.
3. I have translated this and other texts to bring out their meaning for modern readers. Some renderings will differ from traditional ones.
4. See my book *Big Bang, Small Voice*, Whittles, Latheronwheel, Caithness, 1999, reprinted with corrections 2003. Distributor: bmdpgn@amserve.com
5. See, e.g., James B. Pritchard (ed.), *Ancient Near Eastern Texts*, Princeton University Press, 2nd edn., 1955, pp. 60–72.
6. YHWH is the Hebrew name for God. It should probably be pronounced "Yahweh", and means "he who is". Jews have long regarded the name as being too holy to pronounce, saying "my ruler" (*'adhōnāy*) instead. The Greek translators substituted "Ruler" (*Kurios*). (The traditional rendering of *'adhōnāy* and *Kurios* is "Lord", but this has become a weak word in modern English, and "Ruler" is more accurate.)

Chapter 6: Guidance for living?

1. Jesus lived during the Roman empire. His name in Aramaic (his native tongue) was *Yeshū'*, in Greek *Iēsous*, in Latin *Jesus*.
2. Early manuscripts are in Greek. For a listing, see www.kchanson.com/ANCDOCS/greek/papyri.html
3. On this exception, see my book *Jesus's Teaching on Divorce and Sexual Morality*, Whittles, Latheronwheel, Caithness, 2nd edn., 1996, pp. 21–23. Distributor: bmdpgn@amserve.com

4. On my translation of *agapaō* and *miseō* see pp. 42–43.
5. See *Jesus's Teaching on Divorce and Sexual Morality*, pp. 23–24.
6. This passage does not appear in early manuscripts, and is thought either to have been excised or to be a piece of oral tradition that was incorporated later.
7. *Qur'an* 2:224–232, 236–237, 241; 33:49; 65:1–7.
8. *Qur'an* 2:190–193, 216–217, 244; 4:74–76, 84, 104; 8:38–39, 65; 9:5–6, 12–16, 29, 123; 22:39–41; 47:4.

Chapter 7: Help for living

1. The words "pain" and "illness" have traditionally been understood metaphorically as "sorrow" and "grief".
2. *Qur'an* 4:157–158.
3. See Chapter 5, note 6.

Chapter 8: Further teaching

1. I discuss this further in the next chapter.
2. Cf. *Jesus's Teaching on Divorce and Sexual Morality*, Chap. 1.

Chapter 9: Variations

1. Cf. Mary R. Lefkowitz and Maureen B. Fant, *Women's Life in Greece and Rome*, Duckworth, London, 1982, Translation 258 (a tribute to a high priestess). For a full discussion, see my article at www.biblicalstudies.org.uk/pdf/women_nelson.pdf

2. Elie Halévy, *A History of the English People*, Vol. 3, *1830–1841*, tr. E.I. Watkin, Fisher Unwin, London, 1927, p. 166.